BEEN IN THE STORM SO LONG

BEEN
IN THE
STORM
SO LONG

◆ EDITED BY ◆

MARK MORRISON-REED & JACQUI JAMES

Dan Morrison-Reed

To Susan with Best Wishes

BOSTON
SKINNER HOUSE BOOKS

All biblical passages are from the New Revised Standard Version
of the Holy Bible © 1989, Oxford University Press, Division
of Christian Education of the National Council of Churches of
Christ in the United States of America. We are grateful for
permission from McGraw-Hill, Inc., to reprint the excerpt from
Whitney Young, Jr.'s *To Be Equal* © 1964 on page 16. Margaret
Williams Braxton's piece, "Some Day," on page 12 was previously
titled "A Feary Tale." "The Singing of Angels," on page 38, is
from *Meditations of the Heart*, Friends United Press, Richmond,
IN © 1976. Used by permission of The Howard Thurman Educational Trust. "The Work of Christmas," on page 47, is from
The Mood of Christmas, Friends United Press, Richmond, IN ©
1985. Used by permission of The Howard Thurman Educational
Trust.

ISBN 1-55896-202-6
978-1-55896-202-6

Printed in USA

Design by Suzanne Morgan

6 5 4 3 2
09 08 07 06

I've been in the storm so long, children
Been in the storm so long
I've been in the storm so long, children
Gimme a little time to pray.

AFRICAN AMERICAN SPIRITUAL

CONTENTS

THE CONTRIBUTORS

MARJORIE BOWENS-WHEATLEY is program officer for the North Shore Unitarian Universalist Veatch Program and a member of the Unitarian Universalist Fellowship of Huntington, NY.

MARGARET WILLIAMS BRAXTON is a music therapist and a member of the Arlington Street Church in Boston.

THE REV. EGBERT ETHELRED BROWN (1875-1956) was the first African American to be ordained as a Unitarian minister, in 1912. He went on to found churches in Kingston, Jamaica, and Harlem, NY.

THE REV. JEFFREY WORTHINGTON CAMPBELL (1910-1984) became a Universalist minister in 1935 and a Unitarian minister in 1938. He ran for governor of Massachusetts in 1938 on the Socialist ticket.

DR. ERROLD D. COLLYMORE (1893-1972), a dentist and social activist, served as president of the Community Unitarian Church of White Plains, NY, and on the American Unitarian Association's Board of Trustees.

MARGUERITE CAMPBELL DAVIS (1916-1983) was raised as a Universalist in New England. She spent the last 33 years of her life serving the Universalist Church of America and, after 1961, the Unitarian Universalist Association in various administrative capacities. She was the sister of Jeffrey Campbell.

DR. DAVID H. EATON has served as the Senior Minister of All Souls' Unitarian Church in Washington, DC, since 1969. He was president of the Board of Education in Washington, DC, from 1982 to 1985 and is currently an at-large representative on the Board.

HENRY HAMPTON, the executive producer of the critically acclaimed PBS series *Eyes on the Prize*, served as Director of Information and Publicity for the Unitarian Universalist Association from 1963 to 1968 but, by his own account, never quite became a Unitarian Universalist.

FRANCES ELLEN WATKINS HARPER (1825-1911), an abolitionist, poet, lecturer, and "womanist," was a member of the First Unitarian Church of Philadelphia.

THE REV. MELVIN HOOVER is Advocate for Racial Inclusiveness and Director for International Congregations for the Unitarian Universalist Association.

DR. MWALIMU IMARA became a Unitarian Universalist minister in 1968 and served Unitarian Universalist congregations in Urbana, IL, and Boston, MA. He is now an Episcopalian and a professor at the Morehouse School of Medicine in Atlanta.

JACQUI JAMES is Director of Worship Resources and Affirmative Action Officer for the Unitarian Universalist Association.

THE REV. CHARLES JOHNSON is founding minister of the Church of the Restoration, Unitarian Universalist, in Tulsa, OK.

DR. WILLIAM R. JONES, a theologian and educator, is Director of Black Studies and a professor of religion at Florida State University in Tallahassee. Jones has served on the Unitarian Universalist Association's Ministerial Fellowship Committee and the Unitarian Universalist Service Committee Board.

LEWIS H. LATIMER (1848-1928)—inventor, patent expert, draftsperson, engineer, author, poet, and musician—was one of the founding members of the Unitarian Church of Flushing, NY. The son of a runaway slave, Latimer worked with Alexander Graham Bell to create the drawings that helped secure the patent for the first telephone.

THE HON. WADE H. McCREE, JR. (1920-1987) was an attorney who served as a judge in the Sixth Circuit Court of Appeals. He was later appointed United States Assistant Solicitor General, the first African American to hold this position. McCree served as vice-moderator of the Unitarian Universalist Association from 1965 to 1966.

THE REV. LEWIS A. McGEE (1893-1979), a minister raised and ordained in the African Methodist Episcopal tradition, was fellowshipped as a Unitarian in 1948. He helped found the predominantly black Free Religious Fellowship in Chicago.

ROSEMARY BRAY McNATT, a writer, works as an editor for *The New York Times Book Review*. She is a member of Community Church of New York and serves on the Committee on Urban Concerns and Ministry of the Unitarian Universalist Association.

DR. MARK MORRISON-REED is currently co-minister of the First Unitarian Congregation of Toronto.

BECKA ROBBINS, a retired librarian, is a member of the First Unitarian Society of Chicago. She is a poet and volunteer teacher.

ANNE G. RUTLEDGE is an educator, writer, and orator who recently retired from an associate professorship at Alabama A&M University in Huntsville.

BETTY BOBO SEIDEN is a member of the First Unitarian Church of Oakland, CA. She has served on Meadville/Lombard Theological School's Board of Trustees and the Independent Study Committee.

DR. YVONNE K. SEON, the first African American woman to be ordained as a Unitarian Universalist minister, is also the founding minister of Sojourner Truth Congregation in Washington, DC.

THE REV. EUGENE SPARROW (1921-1978) was a Unitarian minister, teacher, and social activist. From 1960 to 1962 he served as Director of Field Services in the Midwestern Unitarian Universalist Conference.

DR. THANDEKA is a fellow at the Stanford Humanities Center in Palo Alto. She will soon join the faculty of Williams College, as an assistant professor of religion.

DR. HOWARD THURMAN (1899-1981)—preacher, theologian, and author—was co-founder of the interracial Church for the Fellowship of All People in San Francisco. A liberal Baptist, he served on the Unitarian Commission on Inter-Group Relations and was welcomed as a guest preacher in numerous Unitarian Universalist congregations.

THE REV. TONI VINCENT was a founding member of the Network of Black Unitarian Universalists and served as its president from 1985 to 1990. She is co-convenor of the African American Unitarian Universalist Ministry.

DR. LORETTA F. WILLIAMS served the Unitarian Universalist Association as Director of Social Responsibility from 1980 to 1989. A sociologist and activist, she was the founding chair of the National Interreligious Commission on Civil Rights.

WHITNEY M. YOUNG, JR. (1921-1971) was a social worker, educator, administrator, and activist. He was the Executive Director of the National Urban League from 1961 to 1971.

INTRODUCTION

We want more soul, a higher cultivation of all spiritual faculties. We need more unselfishness, earnestness, and integrity. . . . We need men and women whose hearts are the homes of high and lofty enthusiasm and a noble devotion to the cause of emancipation, who are ready and willing to lay time, talent, and money on the altar of universal freedom.
—Frances Ellen Watkins Harper

Few in number, scattered through time, African Americans have often found themselves standing alone in our religious movement, their voices largely unheard. Yet when brought together here, these voices blend and harmonize. Certain themes emerge and repeat: the self-evidence of human equality, an immediacy to the human search for justice, an understanding that salvation is corporate, life informed by the nearness of death.

African Americans bring to Unitarian Universalism a sense of urgency in response to the black experience of oppression, a hope born of having survived that experience, and a basic life-affirming joy that can transcend many moments of despair. What Unitarian Universalism offers the African American is, as David Eaton, minister of All Souls' Unitarian Church in Washington, DC, has said, "a more vital reservoir of spiritual awareness [and] a deeper spiritual life."

These readings express all this and more. Covering well over a century, the pieces collected here originated in books, sermons, articles, journals, newsletters, and lectures. We have exercised editorial prerogative and, where possible, eliminated language currently understood as sexist. Since much of this material was not intended to be devotional, we have taken some liberty in adapting it for our purposes.

The families of several African Americans of historical significance to our movement have been of invaluable help, and we are extremely grateful to them for providing us with material from their files. We are also grateful to all our colleagues who responded to our appeal to share their writings with us.

We invite you to use this book freely. It contains material for openings and closings, litanies, and—of course—meditations. It is also meant to be an educational resource that will familiarize the reader with a little-known dimension of our history. We offer this book to Unitarian Universalists with a sense of anticipation. We hope it will help make our movement more reflective of the African American experience and, therefore, more culturally inclusive and accessible to all.

MARK MORRISON-REED

JACQUI JAMES

THE BLACK EXPERIENCE

IN HIS CAGE

The lion stalked up and down his cage, turning his huge body with difficulty in the narrow confines. Now and then he paused in his endless routine to stare through the bars. His eyes, great orbs, were flaming coals. They burned into my eyes until I could no longer return the gaze. The long body resumed its pacing. The great muscles stood out, rippling along the tawny hide with every step, like wide waves upon a sea of gold. I could not leave the beast. My eyes fixed upon him as he paced up and down, up and down. Everything was caught and dragged into the dull, rhythmic thump of padded paws. With closed eyes I saw this lithe body roaming the jungle, the fierce eyes mellowed by peace, the long limbs free to stretch luxuriously. The thing before me was a ghost, a tawny skin encasing only a dying heart and an impassioned longing.

MARGUERITE CAMPBELL DAVIS

THE SLAVE MOTHER

Heard you that shriek? It rose
    So wildly on the air.
It seemed as if a burden'd heart
    Was breaking in despair.

Saw you those hands so sadly clasped—
    The bowed and feeble hand—
The shuddering of that fragile form—
    That look of grief and dread?

Saw you the sad, imploring eye?
    Its every glance was pain,
As if a storm of agony
    Were sweeping through the brain.

She is a mother, pale with fear.
    Her boy clings to her side,
And in her kirtle vainly tries
    His trembling form to hide.

He is not hers, although she bore
    For him a mother's pains;
He is not hers, although her blood
    Is coursing through his veins!

He is not hers, for cruel hands
    May rudely tear apart
The only wreath of household love
    That binds her breaking heart.

His love has been a joyous light
    That o'er her pathway smiled,
A fountain gushing ever new,
    Amid life's desert wild.

His lightest word has been a tone
    Of music round her heart
Their lives a steamlet blent in one—
    Oh, Father! must they part?

They tear him from her circling arms,
    Her last and fond embrace.
Oh! never more may her sad eyes
    Gaze on his mournful face.

No marvel, then, these bitter shrieks
    Disturb the listening air;
She is a mother, and her heart
    Is breaking in despair.

FRANCES ELLEN WATKINS HARPER

THE WANDERER

A cold grey sky, a cold grey sea
And a cold grey mist that is chilling me;
A light that burns on the harbor bar
With the dull dim glow of a distant star.
A sky without hope, a sea lacking cheer
And a beckoning light that comes not near;
The lapping of waves, the whisper of foam,
The gloom of night and a distant home.
What love can I feel for the restless sea
When all I love is leaving me!
The creak of a spar, the flap of a sail
Is far from a song since 'tis nearer a wail;
For the home and the friends that are leaving me
As I'm borne away o'er the cold grey sea.
A cold grey sky, a cold grey sea,
A distant land and a light to me
The only trace as I go my way
Of the joys and hopes of yesterday.
And I look on the sea, I turn to the sky
And they answer me life is mystery.

LEWIS H. LATIMER

I CANNOT ACCEPT THE PROPOSITION

I just cannot accept the proposition that some people are better or worse than other people because of their race— whatever it may be. I accept my race and the race of everyone simply as a condition of existence, like height, weight, age, sex, or shoe size. Now this doesn't mean at all that I am blind to the fact that other people may regard race as the most consequential aspect of their being and my being. I have almost a half century of scars, fortunately most of them on my memory and not on my body, to remind me that I live in a racist society. However, I refuse to permit anyone to infect me with the virus of racial pride because I know it would turn out to be a cancer that would destroy my spirit, my physical self, and the world in which I live.

WADE H. McCREE, JR.

I SEE HER FROM TIME TO TIME

Many people left the church, and some for legitimate reasons. A lot left because they could not stand what I am talking to you about this morning.

Something wonderful and beautiful happened in the midst of it all. A woman, 62 years old, came to my office. She was crying, and I went over and held her in my arms.

She said, "I've got to leave the church."

I asked, "Why?"

She said, "I'm just not comfortable anymore. It was all right before, with ministers who were white. There were a few blacks, but now there are too many joining the church. I'm not comfortable anymore. I feel ashamed of myself." She said, "I'm liberal, and I never thought that I could have racist feelings, but I do."

I said, "Well, you can try to change."

She said, "No, I'm too old for that. I can't change. When I go to church I want to be comfortable. But I'll send you money every now and then to help the church out." And she left.

I see her from time to time. She is out in one of the suburban churches. I see her through the corner of my eye. And if she sees me before I see her, she vanishes quickly. And I let her. But if I see her first, she smiles and we hug each other. She asks me how things are and we quickly part. But I appreciate her honesty.

DAVID H. EATON

FEARS

He phoned more than an hour ago, to say he was on his
way home. But I have yet to hear the scrape of the iron gate,
the rattling keys, so I worry.

Most married women fret about a tardy husband. Young
black women like myself worry more. For most people in
New York the urban bogeyman is a young black man in
sneakers. But we live in Central Harlem, where every young
man is black and wears sneakers, so we learn to look into
the eyes of young males and discern the difference between
youthful bravado and the true dangers of the streets.

No, I have other fears. I fear white men in police uni-
forms; white teenagers driving by; thin, panicky, middle-
aged white men on the subway. Most of all, I fear that their
path and my husband's will cross one night as he makes his
way home.

I fear that some white person will look at him and see
only his or her nightmare—another black man in sneakers.
But he's also a writer, an amateur cyclist, a lousy basketball
player, his parents' son, my life's companion. When I peek
out the window, the visions in my head are those of blind
white panic at my husband's black presence.

Once upon a time I was vaguely ashamed of my paranoia
about his safety in the world outside our home. After all,
he's a grown man. But he's a grown black man on the streets
alone. I am reminded, over and over, how dangerous white
people can be, how their fears are still a hazard to our health.
When white people are ruled by their fears of everything
black, every black man is a rapist—even a murderer.

ROSEMARY BRAY McNATT

DARK AND LIGHT, LIGHT AND DARK

Blackmail, blacklist, black mark. Black Monday, black mood, black-hearted. Black plague, black mass, black market.

Good guys wear white, bad guys wear black. We fear black cats, and the Dark Continent. But it's okay to tell a white lie, lily-white hands are coveted, it's great to be pure as the driven snow. Angels and brides wear white. Devil's food cake is chocolate; angel's food cake is white!

We shape language and we are shaped by it. In our culture, white is esteemed. It is heavenly, sun-like, clean, pure, immaculate, innocent, and beautiful. At the same time, black is evil, wicked, gloomy, depressing, angry, sullen. Ascribing negative and positive values to black and white enhances the institutionalization of this culture's racism.

Let us acknowledge the negative connotations of whiteness. White things can be soft, vulnerable, pallid, and ashen. Light can be blinding, bleaching, enervating. Conversely, we must acknowledge that darkness has a redemptive character, that in darkness there is power and beauty. The dark nurtured and protected us before our birth.

Welcome darkness. Don't be afraid of it or deny it. Darkness brings relief from the blinding sun, from scorching heat, from exhausting labor. Night signals permission to rest, to be with our loved ones, to conceive new life, to search our hearts, to remember our dreams. The dark of winter is a time of hibernation. Seeds grow in the dark, fertile earth.

The words black and dark don't need to be destroyed or ignored, only balanced and reclaimed in their wholeness. The words white and light don't need to be destroyed or ignored, only balanced and reclaimed in their wholeness. Imagine a world that had only light—or dark. We need both. Dark and light. Light and dark.

JACQUI JAMES

SOME DAY

Once upon a time I was
Now I am
Some day I will become

Once there was
And now there is
Soon there will be
And some day there surely shall be

Once upon a time we were
Now we are
And some day (Hallelujah!) we shall surely become

Amen
Amen

MARGARET WILLIAMS BRAXTON

SEEDS OF CHANGE

DREAM IT

I am given to talking about dreams because dreaming separates us from other animals, other life forms. I have a favorite line from a play I read years ago, a Chaucerian drama. The line goes: "In dreams begins responsibility." And indeed it's true. When you dream of something, you can begin to take it upon yourself, make it yours, change it. But you have to dream it first. And the Unitarian Universalists don't dream. . . . You have to think of the world as you would really have it. I don't mean wish it, I mean *dream* it. And sometimes I think Unitarian Universalists wish more than they dream.

HENRY HAMPTON

TRANSCENDING BOUNDARIES

When I was a child, I would stand and gaze at the starry firmament and contemplate infinity. As I stood there, the boundary that is time dissolved; I expanded my Spirit to fill the boundary that is space. My being stilled and all fear, anxiety, and anguish disappeared. Forgotten were the chores, the homework, the ordinary around me.

Transcending boundaries was fun in those days. But, as I reached adulthood, it became more difficult. More and more, the world was with me as I did chores and homework. More and more, my own fears were with me as I encountered others. More and more, I was aware of the boundaries of race, class, age, and sex. I felt myself cringe as the bantering youth in the street came nearer. I felt myself become tearful as I encountered a senior citizen living with pain or the limited choices of a fixed income. I felt myself become angry as I was subjected to the indignities of being rejected by others because I am Black, because I am a woman, or because of the blind person or the openly gay person I was with. I felt myself become unwilling to acknowledge my oneness with the addicted person who is my friend or the homeless people sleeping on the benches in the park.

Today, transcending boundaries is hard work. For one thing, I've created more of them since I was young, and I've built them higher and stronger than they once were. For another thing, I'm much more self-righteous and much less humble than I was then. Sometimes, when I am at my best, I remember that the "other" I distinguish myself from could be me in another time, another place, another circumstance. Then, I remember the words of a colleague who observed that it is "my racism, my sexism, my homophobia" that I am called upon to address. So, I take a few deep breaths and begin to release the fears that are the boundaries between me and my fellow humans.

YVONNE SEON

A LITANY OF RESTORATION

If, recognizing the interdependence of all life,
we strive to build community,
the strength we gather will be our salvation.

If you are black and I am white,
   IT WILL NOT MATTER.

If you are female and I am male,
   IT WILL NOT MATTER.

If you are older and I am younger,
   IT WILL NOT MATTER.

If you are liberal and I am conservative,
   IT WILL NOT MATTER.

If you are straight and I am gay,
   IT WILL NOT MATTER.

If you are Christian and I am Jewish,
   IT WILL NOT MATTER.

If we join spirits as brothers and sisters,
the pain of our aloneness will be lessened . . .
and that does matter.

IN THIS SPIRIT, WE BUILD COMMUNITY
AND MOVE TOWARD RESTORATION.

MARJORIE BOWENS-WHEATLEY

THE CHURCH MUST DECIDE

Instead of an asset, religion has been a liability in the struggle for social reform. The Church, until recently, anesthetized one of the major forces of social change: the American conscience. It provided people with a place where they could congregate regularly in a beautiful setting to hear pious platitudes and mouth meaningless clichés. Then it turned them loose to discriminate against their fellow [humans] the other six and nine-tenths days of the week. Eleven to twelve A.M. on Sundays has been the most segregated hour in America, and it has been easier to integrate the chorus line of a burlesque show than to integrate a choir in most of our churches.

The Church must decide what it is going to do and what it is going to be. Is it a physical plant or is it a social institution? Is the ministry a profession where practitioners are more concerned with the facial expressions of their largest contributors than with helping their congregations to live up to the teachings of the Scriptures? Will ministers only reflect the congregation, will they merely mirror the prejudices of the congregation, or will they mold and lead their congregation?

WHITNEY M. YOUNG, JR.

IT'S HARD WORK

For just as the body without the spirit is dead, faith without works is also dead.

—James 2:26

Why are we still talking about inclusivity and diversity when we have done so little to make them real? Why are we still looking pained about the lack of diversity in the denomination? Because diversity, inclusivity, is terribly hard, terribly uncomfortable, definitely unsettling, and often quite frustrating.

What I know about being inclusive—crossing from culture to culture, learning the language of diversity—is that it's the work of a lifetime. It's hard to accept people who are not like you, who don't talk the way you do, or believe the things you believe, or dress or vote as you do. It's even harder to appreciate them for the things about them that are not like you, to find them interesting and fun, to enjoy the learning that's part of the experience, and to acknowledge, finally, that you may have to agree to disagree.

The truth is this: If there is no justice, there will be no peace. We can read Thoreau and Emerson to one another, quote Rilke and Alice Walker and Howard Thurman, and think good and noble thoughts about ourselves. But if we cannot bring justice into the small circle of our own individual lives, we cannot hope to bring justice to the world. And if we do not bring justice to the world, none of us is safe and none of us will survive. Nothing that Unitarian Universalists need to do is more important than making justice real—here, where we are. Hard as diversity is, it is our most important task.

ROSEMARY BRAY McNATT

BY LOVING

For I was hungry and you gave me food, I was thirsty and you gave me something to drink, I was a stranger and you welcomed me, I was naked and you gave me clothing, I was sick and you took care of me, I was in prison and you visited me. . . . Truly I tell you, just as you did it to one of the least of those who are members of my family, you did it to me.

—Matthew 25:35-40

Throughout ancient tradition and in Jewish and Christian Scriptures emphasis is placed on charity to all, including strangers. Whether faith in Christ is presumed as a prerequisite for facing the final judgment or whether emphasis is strictly on the value of good deeds, the importance of good deeds in all pursuits of life is underscored by Jesus. This description signifies the ultimate commandment to all of us to engage in a personal ministry with every other creature of creation.

To me, one's religion is expressed in the manner in which one relates to other human beings. If one fights relentlessly against injustice, want, hate, and every form of exploitation, then one is a religious person. The love of God is not expressed by ritual or ceremony, but by loving.

WADE H. McCREE, JR.

THE LEGACY OF CARING

Despair is my private pain
    Born from what I have failed to say
        failed to do
        failed to overcome.
Be still my inner self
        let me rise to you
        let me reach down into your pain
        and soothe you.
I turn to you
        to renew my life
I turn to the world
        the streets of the city
            the worn tapestries of
                brokerage firms
                crack dealers
                private estates
                personal things in the bag lady's cart
        rage and pain in the faces that turn from me
            afraid of their own inner worlds.
This common world I love anew
        as the life blood of generations
            who refused to surrender their humanity
            in an inhumane world
            courses through my veins.
From within this world
    my despair is transformed to hope
    and I begin anew
    the legacy of caring.

THANDEKA

SPIRIT OF THE MOMENT

Here in this holy place, on this day of fading Summer and beckoning Fall, let us give ourselves to the Spirit of the moment and find the Sacred Oneness which binds all life together.

Knowing that much is beyond our ability to change, life calls us still to act in compassion and fairness wherever the opportunity presents itself.

Let us seize the strength of the ritual; remember, renew, and relive the taste of hard-fought struggles in the human search for justice.

We are hungry for the lessons of the past and for guidance toward the promise of the future. May we be open to all that expands our awareness, and welcome all to enter our embrace. Amen.

TONI VINCENT

AFFIRMATION OF HOPE

We, bearers of the dream, affirm that a new vision of hope
is emerging.

    We pledge to work for that community in which justice
    will be actively present.

We affirm that there is struggle yet ahead.

    Yet we know that in the struggle is the hope for the
    future.

We affirm that we are co-creators of the future, not passive
pawns.

    And we stand united in affirmation of our hope and
    vision of a just and inclusive society.

We affirm the unity of all persons:

    We affirm brotherhood and sisterhood that allows us to
    touch upon each other's humanity.

We affirm a unity that opens our eyes, ears, and hearts to
see the different but common forms of oppression, suffering, and pain.

    Yet we are one in the image of God, and we celebrate
    our hopes for human unity. Within ourselves and
    within the gathered community, we will discover the
    strength not to hide in indifference.

Affirming that hope, publicly expressed, energizes and
enables us to move forward. Together we pledge action
to transcend barriers—be they racial, political, economic,
social, or religious.

    We pledge to make our tomorrows become our todays.

LORETTA F. WILLIAMS

WHAT WE'VE STARTED

We are here today because we want our religious journey to include more than one holy land, more than one vision, more than one scripture. . . .

We sing praises in many styles and in many languages. We make a joyful noise unto whomever nourishes and sustains all life.

When we look around us here today we see the beauty of diversity—people of various sizes and shapes, heads of different colors and textures. We see an age span of several generations. We are aware of personality differences, of differences in perspective, of ancestors who represent every continent of our world.

Come let us celebrate our diversity.

Come let us worship together.

BETTY BOBO SEIDEN

THE DREAMER AND THE DREAM

~

PRAYING AND DANCING

Knowing that Dorothy Cotton had been the only woman in Dr. Martin Luther King's inner circle, I asked her to describe that experience. The question was followed by silence. When she spoke, I knew that whatever I heard would be only a glimmer of a much larger light. "Oh, in the beginning they were a bunch of chauvinists. . . ." She went on to recount how she would always be the one asked to make the coffee or serve as secretary, though she had as many other duties as the men did.

There was no bitterness in her voice. She immediately followed with an account of what it felt like to be in the eye of that storm. "I don't think people know how much fun it was to work with Dr. King. Singing . . . eating . . . working . . . praying and dancing." What I heard her saying was that love, clarity of intention, and the capacity for joy and celebration are welcome, and necessary, companions in the struggle.

CHARLES JOHNSON

THAT VOICE

No American who has been alive to think and know these last 20 years can ever think of the American Dream without remembering a man who so brought it back to life that thousands of American adults got scared all the way through for fear that he might make them believe it again and they just knew that they couldn't afford it. Whenever they thought about him they just heard that voice thundering off a hill or a big raised platform until you thought it might actually come down from some place so high that most folks didn't go there very often.

And the way he talked made you wonder if you hadn't become a little kid again because he said that he saw people loving and friends and working and playing together as if nothing had happened (would happen) except that they'd go on being friends. It really got creepy. Nobody was used to it yet it sounded so simple and people got uncomfortable-like but then the outside world got more excited about what this man said and kept telling us.

Sometimes he got people to loving so that they didn't mind the dogs the police used on 'em. He won strikes, he led marches, he got new laws passed that gave the Bill of Rights fresh applications, and barriers of hate went down in lots of places where nobody ever thought they would. What he did was so beautiful that I guess some folks couldn't stand it. One of the Big Shot Law and Order Guys even got so he'd get messages sent to this man with ideas about killing himself. They'd sent his wife letters saying, "Your man is screwing around." But nothing seemed to stop him.

He just talked about not hating until I guess people, some people, couldn't take it so somebody shot him and things quieted down. Some Americans said that when they went abroad to other countries, some people looked at them funny-like and didn't say anything. But perhaps that's because it wasn't their country.

JEFFREY WORTHINGTON CAMPBELL

A FALLEN FRIEND

Great Spirit of light and of darkness:
We gather once again to remember a fallen friend,
    and nourish ourselves from the fountain of reflections.
Open our hearts to the anguish of our pain,
    to the tired taste of swallowed tears,
    and to our unrealized vision.

In this place we bring our scattered lives together,
    groping for meaning and looking for truth.
Be with us as we continue our search for understanding of
    the mystery of the temporal.
Stay with us as we wander through our memories,
    seeking pathways to the future.
Move with us as we unravel the implied imperatives of
    hopes unfulfilled.

Justice makes tireless demands, and we grow weary.
As we touch one another in common cause,
    and with the great spirit in our midst,
Let us find the way and the courage to realize the dream
    which still lives within us. Amen.

TONI VINCENT

I COME NOT TO PRAISE KING

I have come not to praise King, but to criticize him.

I have come to the agonizing conclusion that to justly honor King at this time and to place him in our history and advance the goal for which he joyously lived and courageously died, we must pinpoint the real defects in his thought.

Why this bewildering way of praising King? The most important reason is the ideological abuse of King's deeds and doctrine by those who want to negate his dream. To be truthful, we would have to admit that King has become, as it were, the black messiah, the singular and exclusive pattern not only for blacks in America to imitate but also for other liberation movements throughout the world. Black leaders are indexed as militant or violent, not on the basis of their actual thoughts and deeds but by virtue of how far they strayed from King's footsteps.

I have a nagging suspicion that white America desires to perpetuate a black hero who fits its special needs of oppression and not those of black liberation. White adoration of King secures him more as a guardian of white interest than as a black Moses to lead his people to freedom.

How then should we praise this black hero? Difficult though it may be, we must finally be able to say in the words of one of his colleagues, "We've never buried Dr. King, and we won't be able to do anything until we do." His dream will only become a reality, it appears, when black and white Americans can say—and with conviction—"King is dead, long live the King." His life and thought must be acknowledged as giant steps in the march to black freedom. But we dishonor him if we think that his way is the only path that we who aim to be free must follow. We shall not overcome if we march only to his beat as the distant drummer and ignore the stout cadence of others in the army of black thought and action.

WILLIAM R. JONES

SPIRIT OF THE PIONEER

We can't change the past, but we can learn from it and build on it.

We can't control the future, but we can shape it and enhance the possibilities for our children and grandchildren.

We can't discern in the present the fullness of our actions and their impact, but we can be pioneers in our time, exploring fully the crevices and cracks where knowledge and new insights might be found.

We can explore our spectrum of relationships and confront our complacency and certainty about the way things are.

We can dare to face ourselves in our entirety,
    to understand our pain,
    to feel the tears,
    to listen to our frustration and confusion, and
    to discover new capacities and capabilities that
        will empower and transform us.
In the spirit of the pioneer, let us now go forth.

MELVIN HOOVER

VOICES LIFTED

A FAITH TO WORK BY

I must confess that for me the pace has been slow. The gains have been small in my quest for God, my quest for a faith. I am still far from the goal. But still I seek.

Out of all the tragedy and the doubt, I do believe that I emerged perhaps one step forward. From experience I know that there are contrasts in living—and of these contrasts there can be found *a good life*. A life of peace, of goodwill, of decency . . . of love, of harmony, and of beauty. The attributes of a good life can be attained by the conscious will and desire of the individual.

This conscious effort to achieve the good life might be considered a religion. *I can share in a religion like this.*

Personally, I want a religion to live by. I want a faith to work by.

ERROLD D. COLLYMORE

SIN BROUGHT ME BACK

Sin is what caused me to leave the church and give up religion, and sin is what brought me back.

In my grandmother's house, sin was associated with pleasure. All those things that I thought were fun were of the world, and therefore sinful. Dancing, playing cards, going to the movies all condemned me to Hell—which made it sound like a pretty interesting place. In my father's house, sin was associated with form and ritual. Eating meat on Friday, coming into church with the head uncovered— these were misdeeds to confess. But I couldn't feel guilty about them.

Years later my three-year-old son came running to the house to tell me that a neighbor's boy had just told him that God would kill him if he told a lie. I decided that it was time we found a religious community that would sustain and encourage our beliefs:

> that we are part of a universe of diversity and
> interdependence,
> that the diversity of our world suggests that truth
> and beauty take many forms,
> that God is concerned with the enhancement of life,
> that evil is life-destroying,
> that sin is associated with self-absorption, and
> that salvation lies in selflessness and service.

A religious community is *in* the world and concerned with the world.

BETTY BOBO SEIDEN

WE MAY HAVE IT!

Millions upon millions of people everywhere are drifting from the old formulations, no longer willing to view the ancient myths as religious truths. They are looking for a vital, modern religion with a personal and social imperative. We may have it! I think we do!

Our religion is a religion of social concern, a religion of intellectual and ethical integrity, a religion that emphasizes the dynamic conception of history and the scientific world-view, a religion that stresses the dignity and worth of the person as a supreme value and goodwill as the creative force in human relations. This religion can and ought to become a beacon from which this kind of faith shines.

LEWIS A. McGEE

THE GOD WITHIN

Those who deny God deny themselves. For God, in a mystical sense beyond the power of words to express, is within all of us.

The past years have deepened my belief that God is within, working in mysterious ways. I therefore believe profound introspection is a synonym for prayer. But it is not just an arid exercising of the intellect, a scientific analysis of one's inner nature. Genuine emotion also plays a role in the religious experience. The world and its people, despite differences in definition of objectives, have begun to reach toward the spirit of love.

I believe the love of one's fellow humans is not just a passive intellectual concern for their welfare. Such love should manifest itself as an active effort to improve their lot. The renaissance for human dignity is moving forward, helping not only the oppressed but also the oppressor to find the God within.

EUGENE SPARROW

COLD SERVICES

Religion is ethics touched by emotion. If the intellect dominates and there is no hint of emotion, a cold and barren matter-of-factness results. Conversely, if emotion leads, unguided by intellect, we are doomed to a wild sea of fanaticism. Yet mind and soul united create one music, grander than before.

Have you ever been emotionally moved as you sat at your desk preparing a sermon? Have you ever been blinded by tears you dared not shed? I have. And I remember those sermons as my best—precisely because I preached them to myself before I preached them to others.

Cold services! There will be no such thing when more of our sermons are messages wrought from our deepest experiences of joy and sorrow, messages that first warmed and stirred our own souls.

EGBERT ETHELRED BROWN

SONGS FOR THE PEOPLE

Let me make the songs for the people,
　Songs for the old and young;
Songs to stir like a battle-cry
　Wherever they are sung.

Not for the clashing of sabres,
　Nor for carnage nor for strife;
But songs to thrill the hearts of [all]
　With more abundant life.

Let me make the songs for the weary,
　Amid life's fever and fret,
Till hearts shall relax their tension,
　And careworn brows forget.

Let me sing for little children,
　Before their footsteps stray,
Sweet anthems of love and duty,
　To float o'er life's highway.

I would sing for the poor and aged,
　When shadows dim their sight;
Of the bright and restful mansions,
　Where there shall be no night.

Our world, so worn and weary,
　Needs music, pure and strong,
To hush the jangle and discords
　Of sorrow, pain, and wrong.

Music to soothe all its sorrow,
    Till war and crime shall cease;
And the hearts of [all] grown tender
    Girdle the world with peace.

FRANCES ELLEN WATKINS HARPER

WITHOUT LOVE

As we face a troubled and puzzled world, we too are troubled and puzzled. As our fond dreams remain unrealized and our bright hopes of yesterday wither in the bitter disappointments of today, our courage fails, our spirits droop, our faith trembles, and, frustrated, we bow our heads in despair.

Nevertheless, we come to God in this hour of worship, in this house of prayer.

As we pray for peace in our time, O God, may we ourselves be at peace with the world, with ourselves, and with Thee. May we know that without love there will never be peace. Teach us therefore to love. What does this world need more than love?

May we, after hearing the message of the day, leave this place inspired and strengthened, faithfully to fulfill the duties of tomorrow.

EGBERT ETHELRED BROWN

MUST JESUS BEAR THE CROSS ALONE?

Some of you have heard me say, "Don't take Jesus away from me!" You may have thought this strange coming from a Unitarian Universalist minister. But, when I say this, I don't mean Jesus, a Being whose perfection removes him from most of us in this realm. I mean Jesus, the human person, like me; Jesus, capable of divine inspiration, insight, and response, like me; Jesus, responsible, like me, for creating change, here, now! In liberation theology, Jesus bears the cross as a powerful symbol that we each have a share in bearing the crosses of life, and that we all have the capacity to transcend the pain of our crosses to achieve a higher life of meaning. "Must Jesus bear the cross alone, and all the world go free? No, there's a cross for everyone; and there's a cross for you and for me!" Amen.

YVONNE SEON

THE SINGING OF ANGELS

There must be always remaining in every life some place for the singing of angels, some place for that which in itself is breathlessly beautiful and—by an inherent prerogative, throwing all the rest of life into a new and creative relatedness—something that gathers up in itself all the freshets of experience from drab and commonplace areas of living and glows in one bright light of penetrating beauty and meaning, then passes. The commonplace is shot through with new glory, old burdens become lighter, deep and ancient wounds lose much of their old, old hurting. A crown is placed over our heads that for the rest of our lives we are trying to grow tall enough to wear. Despite all the crassness of life, despite all the hardness of life, despite all the harsh discords of life, life is saved by the singing of angels.

HOWARD THURMAN

TO EVERYTHING
A SEASON

LOVE IS ALL

What is there in this world, beside our loves,
To keep us here?
Ambition's course is paved with hopes deferred,
With doubt and fear.
Wealth brings no joy,
And brazen-throated fame
Leaves us at last
Nought but an empty name.
Oh soul, receive the truth,
E'er heaven sends thy recall:
Nought here deserves our thought but love,
For love is all.

LEWIS H. LATIMER

INFINITY

Infinity is indicated
In fingerprints
In stars
In grasses, leaves, heads of hair
In sands, raindrops, flakes of snow
In flower seeds
Bird's feathers
Rushing rivers
Unceasing thoughts and dreams.

The presence of good is indicated
In blue of sky
In green of earth
In thus-far of waves
In still of heights
In cool of shade
In wafting of wind
Breaking of bread
Transcendence of love.

BECKA ROBBINS

LET ME DIE LAUGHING

We are all dying, our lives always moving toward completion.

We need to learn to live with death, and to understand that death is not the worst of all events.

We need to fear not death, but life—

empty lives,

loveless lives,

lives that do not build upon the gifts that each of us have been given,

lives that are like living deaths,

lives that we never take the time to savor and appreciate,

lives in which we never pause to breathe deeply.

What we need to fear is not death, but squandering the lives we have been miraculously given.

So let me die laughing, savoring one of life's crazy moments. Let me die holding the hand of one I love, and recalling that I tried to love and was loved in return. Let me die remembering that life has been good, and that I did what I could. But today, just remind me that I am dying so that I can live, savor, and love with all my heart.

MARK MORRISON-REED

THE MESSAGE

Let us rejoice that we are alive today, privileged to meet here in quest of life's meaning. The message in this season of renewal is that life is a precious gift of nature, to be lived at its best, to be enjoyed and wisely used. There is a structure to life related to the natural universe, whose laws cannot be violated with impunity—a structure related to other life around us. Those who grapple courageously with the events of life will get more joy out of living. Those who so appreciate life and are living on the high plane are ready to die at any time. The death of the individual is the price we pay for being, but the eternal life stream flows on from generation to generation.

LEWIS A. McGEE

THE GRIEF OF SUDDEN LOSS

The human spirit has an enormous resiliency, but it is pushed to its limits by the grief that follows sudden, meaningless, violent deaths. It is one thing to sit beside someone you love who is dying from an advancing illness. The death will hurt. We will grieve. We will go through that tortuous journey of many months until somehow the scattered pieces of our soul again blend and our life moves forward from the painful shadows. For at a deeper level, there is a logic here that we can understand and accept.

But senseless, violent death not only violates our sense of cosmic justice but generates an outrage that defies all time's healing. The feelings of abandonment in the intense grief following such deaths remove much of our positive sense of self. Our self-esteem, our sense of worth, dissolves in the pain.

Yet, when someone is willing to listen and not shrink from our untidy suffering—our raging at family, at God, and at ourselves—their esteem for us begins to repair our own lack of self-regard. Here is the healing support we need to struggle with the suffering.

We can survive the intensity of impossible losses because our very spirit is designed by God to survive the strain, if we have the resources to enable us to bear the pain. A major resource is communion with our companions in the struggle. Our spirit's healing temple is someone's available, understanding heart. Some call this place the "Holy of Holies." I pray that all who struggle with the pain of grief from sudden, violent death will find the faith and communal support to grow through it to wholeness.

MWALIMU IMARA

THE BELIEVER

What is it to believe
that out of Nothing-ness
has come
a Being whose Ending
is as the Beginning—

An Entity from Nowhere
on an unalterable course

All-seeing
    All-knowing
        All-flowing

out of Nowhere
into No-Time
into Nothing-ness.

What is it to deny
the implausibility
of Knowing

the Maker of the Stars
the Moon/the Sun of
the Universe/where Other
Forms of life look down

in pity
    or mirth/

Is it the curl of a leaf
as it turns and waits
for Another Life
Or is it the dissent
of the grass/as it weeps
beneath/relentless feet/
Or the petal
of the rose

Dying/
while I am dying?

Life is a comma
where we pause/
on our Way
    to Somewhere Else/

Death is a . . . Period . . .

    Period.

ANNE G. RUTLEDGE

A COMMON DESTINY

All living substance, all substance of Energy,
    and Being,
        and Purpose,
are united and share the same destiny.

All people,
    those we love and those we know not of
are united and share the same destiny.

Birth-to-Death
this unity we share with
        the Sun,
        Earth
        our Brothers and Sisters,
        Strangers
        Flowers of the field,
        Snowflakes
        Volcanoes and Moon Beams.

Birth—Life—Death
Unknown—Known—Unknown
Our Destiny: from Unknown to Unknown.

I pray that we will know the Awe
    and not fall into the pit of intellectual arrogance
    in attempting to explain it away.
The Mystery can be our substance.
May we have the faith to accept this wonderful Mystery
    and build upon its everlasting Truth.

DAVID H. EATON

Dedicated to Peg Pierce, January 13, 1974.

THE STAR IN THE SKY

THE WORK OF CHRISTMAS

When the song of the angels is stilled,
When the star in the sky is gone,
When the kings and princes are home,
When the shepherds are back with their flock,
The work of Christmas begins:
 to find the lost,
 to heal the broken,
 to feed the hungry,
 to release the prisons,
 to rebuild the nations,
 to bring peace among the brothers,
 to make music in the heart.

HOWARD THURMAN

THE GIFT

The gift came as silence,
encircling all that we are,
softly settling over
memories of Christmas past:

> The great joy of knowing that we are loved.
> The real knowing—no matter how enlightened
> we've become—visiting us with the touch of a
> warm hand, a shiny new toy, the ever-increasing
> aroma that makes food spell love.

> The irrevocable kinship with earth: a tiny ball
> on the edge of time, a tender openness to being
> finite.

The gift came as love,
the patient willingness to acknowledge that maybe
now is as good as it has ever been, will ever be:

> Certain and satisfied that our parents loved
> us the best they knew how—even in those
> times when they gave up on us or let us go.

> Courage in the discovery of the freedom present in
> "my life . . . my time . . . my love . . . my body."
> Transcending the fear of "my choice."

> Remembering a time when someone trusted a part
> of us we hardly knew ourselves: hearing in the
> whisper of their voice, "You are sufficient to
> the task."

Mercy in the hope that our children will one
day account for our gifts to them, remember us
in honor, then grow into the fullness of their
own lives.

Measuring the distance between my eyes and
those across from me now, not knowing how this
could ever end, and tasting what the poets called
eternity.

A brand-new awareness of old words and
too-soon-forgotten strength drawn from suffering
unearned, believing in its embrace that the
price has already been paid.

Love as knowing we were worth it.

The gift comes as silence:

A sacred time in which hurry doesn't win,
a deep space suitable for the high art of
reflection.

An open and thankful heart
unafraid of pain,
unafraid of the love which is pain's hearth.

Unafraid to call on God, willing to overcome the
fear that nags humankind that we are alone and that
no one will answer.

Willing, in this season, to pause and to be
thankful that we can forgive as easily as we have
been wronged, and that our forgiveness in life
helps the world toward peace.

To remember that the christchild did as we must—
grow up and face destiny . . . that longing inside
which calls us with the certainty that We Must.

> Memories, ideals and longings, invitations and
> repulsions—with joy and tinsel and
> conversation . . . all afforded by the real,
> unchanging gift—this silence, this presence,
> this moment and always.

The great joy in being alive.

The great joy in knowing, this night and as long as we live,
in the bounty and variety of a well-trimmed tree,
that God is with us.

CHARLES JOHNSON